A friendly guide of what to wear, when to wear and how, including tips for hijabis.

WEAR

WHAT

WHEN

Hanifah Ashry

WEAR WHAT WHEN

Copyright © 2020 Hanifah Ashry

All rights reserved.

ISBN: 9798687036153

Published by
It's All About Him Media & Publishing
5201 Nations Ford Road, Ste D
Charlotte, NC 28217
www.aahmp.com
980-522-8096

Chief Editor: Delisa Fields
Cover Designer: Saran Djane
Images courtesy of Pixaby.com and unsplash.com

Bio photo credit: Ferhana Yeasmin

Contact the Author

Website: www.hanifahashry.com

Email: hanifah.ashry@gmail.com

DEDICATION

To my family and friends who have continually supported me over the years and constantly encouraged me to pursue my passions.

To my son, the love of my life, who has made me a better person ever since he came into this world.

TABLE OF CONTENTS

Hanifah Ashry

ACKNOWLEDGMENTS

I want to give a huge thank you to my amazing publisher, Delisa Rodgers-Fields, of It's All About Him Media and Publishing, for guiding me through this process, being so attentive, communicative, and dedicated to seeing this project through as well as my sweet co-worker, Angie, for referring me to her.

A squishy hug and thank you to my graphic designer and little sister, Saran Djane, for being so patient with me, advising me, and creating the cover for my book.

I am also grateful to my friend and former co-worker, Cody, who hyped me up and encouraged me to finally finish this book a few years ago.

I would like to extend my sincere thanks to my wonderful family, friends, and all of the people out there that followed and supported my first fashion blog and fashion consulting business because that is where this all started.

I would not be able to do anything without God. Alhamdullilah for this opportunity, this journey and this knowledge that I have been blessed with that I am able to share with others.

INTRODUCTION

Fashion, to me, is a form of art. It is a form of artistic expression, just like any other art form such as singing, dancing, painting, etc. Fashion is an avenue of self-expression for designers, a way to communicate to the world who they are.

Similarly, style is an avenue of self- expression for an individual through their choice of dress. Of course, in order for this to work, you must have a strong sense of self, or else the purpose is defeated. Some may dress to play a part. That sort of fashion is just clothes on a body, not style. Style is fashion, personalized.

In fashion, designers create stories, concepts, and themes with cohesive collections, including a variety of fabrics, types of garments, etc. Your job, as the consumer, is to buy the garments that will reflect your personal style. My job as a fashion consultant is to help you make that interpretation.

This book will guide you through the world of fashion and help you to make the best, most stylish choices possible for what to wear and when to wear it.

Hanifah Ashry

CHAPTER 1

TOP TEN FASHION MYTHS

Originally, there were just going to be five myths, but there are a few more that I thought were important to mention.

> *A lot of myths surrounding fashion are not true.*

Some of the time, certain fashion "rules" are in place strategically and purposefully so that we can spend a certain way or buy more of a certain product making it more convenient and profitable for businesses. Or they are just something made up that doesn't have great reasons behind it and places limits on things that don't need them.

Now, to reveal the untold truths about some of these myths...

1. *No white (shoes, etc.) after Labor Day.*

Nope, not true. It is perfectly okay to wear white pants, white coats, white shoes, white dresses, etc. after Labor Day. Keep your white garments clean, and you're good to go.

Example:

Would you wear your cute white flats in icy, snowy, slushy weather? No, because you might end up looking gross by the time you reach your destination.

Would you wear a fresh white cocktail dress to an elegant winter holiday party? Yes.

Keep on working the white well after Labor Day but be smart about it.

2. *Shoes and purse and/or belt must match.*

If you want to match your shoes and your purse, go for it! But you don't HAVE to. Mixing it up every now and then can be fun. Try a thin white belt with your black pants, white button-down shirt, and black boots.

Instead of a black purse and black shoes, try black shoes and a silver purse. Metallics, like silver and gold, as well as other colors like yellow, white, and navy blue, can be just as neutral like black and brown and work well for outfits.

Remember, if you decide to match your purse with your shoes, be sure to remember that that means you have already done one color in two significant ways. If you decide to wear more of that color in your ensemble, do it minimally, such as wearing a ring.

3. *Brightly colored clothing and accessories are for spring and summer.*

So not true. Bright colors are fine all year around. When fall and winter roll around, it's hard not to fall into that dreary, hermit mode. Brightly colored purses, coats, dresses, and shoes, etc. in red, purple, pink, yellow, or other bright colors may help your mood and will step up an outfit.

4. *You have to put all of your sleeveless garments and short sleeves away during fall and winter.*

Nope. You can rock those short-sleeved tees, sleeveless shirts, and shorter skirts in the fall and winter. How? Cover up! Put on thin long-sleeved shirts under those tees and sleeveless shirts, or layer cardigans, blazers, and jackets on top of them.

For shorter skirts, throw on a pair of tall boots to keep your legs warm. Thin fabrics will require more layers to keep warm. If layering isn't your thing, then you may want to just stick to garments with warm fabrics.

Hijabs: you've got a leg up on this one because we do this all year around! :)

5. *Tights and sandals look cute together.*

Sorry, they just don't. Tights with sandals were hot in Fall '07 and are trying to make a comeback, but it's still not cute. In fact, it looks tacky. Sandals are for warm weather on purpose. Your toes and feet are meant to be out so that they are not inside a shoe burning up in 70+ degree weather. Wearing tights with sandals doesn't make sandals cold-weather shoes. Just go for a closed-toe boot, bootie, etc., or peep-toe shoes at the most.

However, if you are going to an indoor event in the fall/winter season and you will not have to walk around in the cold, wear those fabulous sandals (without tights.)

6. *Tall women shouldn't wear high heels.*

Absolutely not true. Just because you were born with the gift of height doesn't mean you have to sacrifice a pair of hot heels. You can wear high heels just like anyone else can. If you are uncomfortable wearing high heels, then that's fine. Wear some cute flats, but you do have the option.

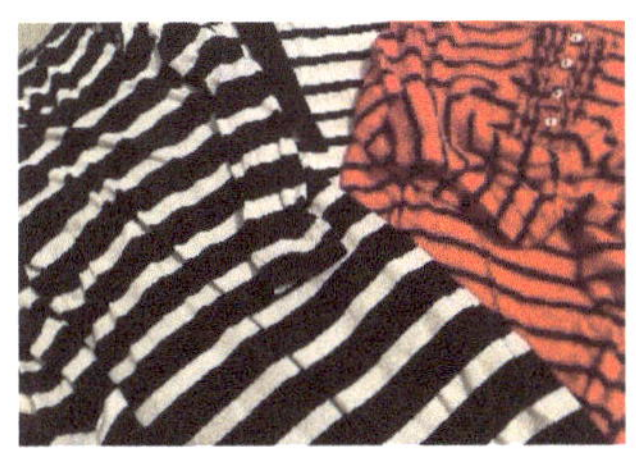

7. *Horizontal stripes make you look larger than you are.*

This is not always true; it depends on the garment. Some garments that have thick bold, or thin horizontal stripes will look just fine. Others that have thick or thin horizontal stripes might look awkward.

The solution... try it on! You can never be sure how something will look on you until you try it on and see what it does for your body.

Thick belts can help break up stripes for a more flattering look.

8. *Gold and silver metallics cannot be mixed or worn at the same time.* That's a myth. You can mix silver and gold without it looking crazy, just try it out and see how it looks.

Example:

Wearing a silver dress with gold heels might look cool. Or, wearing silver hoops and then a gold purse could look awesome. Try it out and see how it looks.

9. You can't wear more than one bold/bright color.

Who says? You can wear more than one bold or bright color in the same ensemble. The key is to choose two colors that complement each other and pair them both with a neutral.

Example:

Royal purple sleeveless dress, and a mustard yellow shirt, with a chocolate brown purse.

Example:

Crimson red tee, a pair of dark wash blue jeans, and blue flats.

10. You can't wear white to a wedding.

I know, I know. This sounds insane. However, you CAN wear white to a wedding. Why? Because not all brides wear white AND you don't have to wear all-white, just a touch of it.

Example:

You can wear a white pencil skirt with a shiny black top, or you can wear a white blazer with a black long straight skirt.

Example:

If you are going to an Indo-Pak wedding, most brides wear red. It is okay to wear an all-white outfit then. Do your research before going to a wedding to keep from looking crazy.

So, go and disprove these myths fabulously!

CHAPTER 2

BABY, ITS COLD OUTSIDE: WHAT TO WEAR IN THE WINTER

So, winter has rolled around, and it's snowy, icy, and bitter cold outside.

What do you wear?

The warmest, most fly things you can find, of course!

Here are a few key pieces and wardrobe elements that you can use to keep yourself looking cute in the cold!

Warm Fabrics

Choosing pieces with thicker warmer fabrics is an excellent way to stay toasty. Fabrics such as denim, velvet, fleece, cashmere, flannel, corduroy, wool, tweed, and furs are all great. Be sure to test the fabrics on your skin to make sure that they will not irritate it.

Long Skirts

Long skirts (ankle length or longer) are going to be great for winter because the extra length goes a long way. Try out different shapes like mermaid, straight, A-line, trumpet, and etc. Rock a long skirt with a top tucked into it.

Hijabis, if the skirt isn't super loose at the top and you want to wear a tucked top, you can just wear a jacket or cardigan over it to keep the goodies covered or just wear the top untucked and try a thin belt if it looks right. Also, put on a great pair of leggings/tights and boots under your long skirts for extra warmth.

Sweaters and Cardigans

Sweaters and cardigans are going to be your best choices for tops in the winter months. Fabulous pieces like thin sweaters and sweater vests, grandfather cardigans, and wrapping cardigans are especially good if you like to dress in layers. Layer your turtlenecks and graphic tees under these pieces.

Hijabis, rock long cardigans with pants and shorter ones with skirts and dresses.

Turtlenecks

Turtlenecks are a great winter wardrobe staple because they are warm and oh, so stylish. Rock a turtleneck in many different colors and/or textures; they are especially useful for layering. You can wear a low-cut top and throw on a turtleneck under it to keep yourself warm and covered. You can still wear your statement necklaces with turtlenecks, just make sure that the jewelry does not get caught on the fabric.

Hijabis, turtlenecks are great for hijab styles that need neck coverage as well.

Leggings and Tights

Leggings and tights are an awesomely easy way to keep your legs warm during the winter. These thin pieces are handy for wearing under most garments such as pants, jeans, long skirts, and dresses for extra insulation. You can also wear your leggings and tights with shorter dresses and skirts paired with boots for warmth and look very cute.

Hijabis, rock your leggings and tights at home or at private events in these ways.

Coats

Coats come in numerous styles, and there are plenty of stylish winter coats out there. Whether it's a puffer, trench-style, fur, or peacoat, pick one that fits your lifestyle and flatters your body and personal style. Also, you can choose a cool color like royal blue or a fun pattern like plaid.

Coats with medium-sized belts are very flattering for all shapes.

Gloves

Gloves are a must to keep the fingers from freezing in the winter. Having more than one pair is a good idea so that you can have options depending on what you are doing that day. There are many styles of gloves to choose from, but some of the most popular styles are insulated leather gloves. If you are going sledding, skiing, or playing in the snow, you may want to skip the fancy leather gloves and go for non-leather thermal gloves. Also, if you are going to a fancy event, you can rock some fabulous satin gloves to step up your outfit.

Scarves

Scarves in fabrics like pashmina and fleece are going to be very warm. Throw a scarf around your neck or across your face to keep the cold out this winter.

Boots

Boots are critical in the winter. In the snow, rain, and ice, warm rubber-soled boots are essential to have. *Can you have the function with the fabulousness?* Of course. Just find a good pair. Thigh-high and knee-high boots with insulation are going to be the best options.

If you are going out in wet weather, it may not be a good idea to wear your heeled boots that do not have rubber soles because you might slip and fall. However, if you have platform/heeled boots with rubber soles, rock those! If it is just bitter cold but pretty dry outside, go for the regular boots.

Hats

Believe it or not, hats are not just for bad hair days. Hats can actually keep your head warm and look super stylish, especially when they match your coat or jacket. For winter, go for hats like berets, cloches, newsboy caps, and skull-cap type hats, etc. in knits and wools for warmth.

CHAPTER 3

FIVE MUST-HAVES FOR SUMMER

<u>MUST-HAVE #1: Maxi Dresses!</u>

Can't talk about summer must-haves and not mention the coveted maxi dress! A breezy maxi dress in a beautiful color or print paired with sandals or flip flops is perfect for the warm weather.

*The fabric of the dress dictates whether it is for day or evening wear, the occasion for which it would be appropriate.

<u>MUST-HAVE #2: Sun Hats!</u>

Yes, it's a must, especially on the days when the sun is absolutely blazing, and you will be out in it.

A wide sun hat is the icing on the cake for an excellent warm-weather outfit. It adds that extra dash of fabulous like "Yes, Honey!"

Relatively flat or low hair/hijab styles are necessary for wearing hats. Please, also make sure it matches and compliments your outfit.

Can hats be worn inside? Yes, if the occasion calls for it. Some formal events/occasions are big hat friendly.

MUST-HAVE #3: Sunglasses!

Sunglasses, or "Sunnies" as Rachel Zoe says, are an absolute must-have! Why? Because not only will they keep your eyes shaded from the sun, they instantly bump you up in style status. There's something about sunglasses, whether aviator, bug-eye, "Nicole Richie style," and etc., that says, "I'm Fly!"

No makeup today? No Problem! Tired eyes or just feel like being incognito today? No problem.

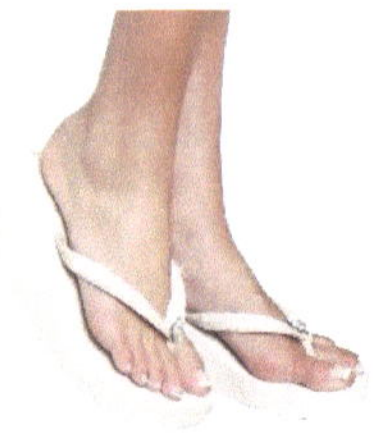

MUST-HAVE # 4: Flip Flops!

Yes, you all, flip flops. But not the dollar store kind that you just use for questionable showers or those cheap pairs to slip your feet in really quick at home. I'm talking about the platform, wedge, or ones with small heels, bejeweled, or printed, relatively quality flip flops.

If you are going to rock flip flops, they have to be right! Why flip flops, though? Cuz it's hot! Sometimes, you want your feet to be able to breathe a little more on really hot days, or you just want a more laid- back, casual yet cute look that's fast and easy.

MUST-HAVE # 5: A Summer Glow

To top off your summer ensemble, you gotta have your summer glow. What do I mean by that? I mean beautiful glowing skin. In the winter, the skin is more prone to dryness, ashy-ness, and dullness due to the weather. However, in the summertime, the sun kisses the skin with a tan, and sometimes the heat makes us sweat, which actually is good to get impurities out, etc.

To get a nice summer glow, keep your skin clean, protected, and moisturized (sunscreen and exfoliation are important.) Lotions and creams with a little shimmer and tint in them are nice as long as they aren't the ones that rub off on everything.

If you wear makeup, illuminating powders, highlighters, and soft blushes are good as well as lightweight foundations and powders that match your skin color to enhance your natural beauty. Also, remember that lovely skin begins with the inside, so drink lots of water and eat healthy.

CHAPTER 4

HIJABIS AT HOME: HOW TO LOOK PRETTY IN PRIVATE

So, you can look just as cute at home or at a private event as you do when you go outside.

The same effort or more should be made so that you don't let yourself go, even when you think you will not be "seen," because YOU still have to see yourself and feel good about what you see.

Some things like tights or super fitted/short dresses, etc., that are not hijabi-appropriate can be worn by hijabis at home or at private events. Also, if it is cold outside, you can bust out those warm-weather items like lightweight dresses, tees, skirts, and wear them inside where it is warm and cozy.

Now, let's explore the options!

<u>Coverup Options</u>

Wanna cover up a little bit if you don't want to show that much skin and goodies or just in case you get cold? Try throwing on one of these pieces: cropped cardigan, Bolero jacket, hip length cardigan, shrug, shawl, scarf, and long sleeves

Add one of these cover-ups to any of these pieces/ensembles mentioned below based on your comfort level.

<u>Tank Tops</u>

Tank tops or bustier (corset tops) tops are super cute for inside and can be worn with a great fitted pair of jeans or a skirt.

<u>T-Shirts/Tees</u>

No, no! Not those oversized tees that swallow you up or are stained and falling apart. We are talking about cute t-shirts like graphic tees or plain fitted tees. Wear a tee with jeans or a skirt.

Peasant Skirts

Peasant skirts are comfortable and light wearing inside. Wear them long or knee-length, with a cute tank top or tee.

Pencil Skirts

Pencil skirts are hot little skirts that are fitted, high-waisted at times, and fall just below or just above the knee. They look classy and cute especially paired with tops tucked into them with or without a thin belt.

Maxi Dresses

Maxi dresses are very comfortable for inside or private events because they can be very casual or very glamorous with some jewelry and a great hairstyle. They come in such a variety of styles and colors.

Short Dresses

All of those short dresses like minidresses, cocktail dresses, t-shirt dresses, etc. can be worn inside with a pair of skinny jeans, tights, or leggings if you choose.

Gowns

Yes, gowns. At private formal events and for special evenings at home, bust out a gown. It can be one of those fitted, flirty (but tasteful) ones if you want and rock a fabulous hairstyle to boot.

Caftans

Caftans are a super-comfortable option that comes in many different fabrics and styles from various different cultures. Rock a caftan if you are just lounging around the house or for a private party.

Caftans, belted or not belted, with statement earrings and stacked bangles is a fabulous look. The caftans that you find at Ross and Moroccan style caftans are lovely choices.

Cute Sweat Suits

Now, I usually say No to sweat suits being worn other than for the purpose of doing physical exercise. However, if it is a cute sweat suit like the fitted J-Lo or Juicy Couture ones in a great color (even the ones with the sayings on them like "Hottie" lol), then you can wear it in the house. You can also wear them to a sleepover (not at a lady's cocktail party) to be comfy, especially if you're bloaty or pregnant. But don't get used to it and wear it every day... promise? Please.

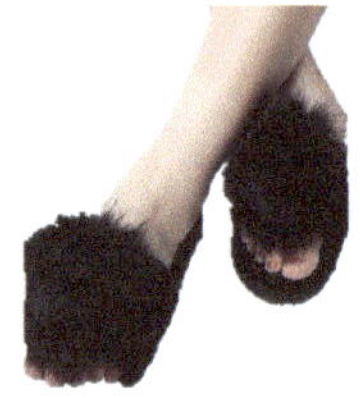

House Shoes
No, not that ratty pair of slippers. Buy a pair of cute shoes/dainty slippers, be it heels or flats, that are made out of relatively soft material as not to mess up your floor or carpet that are ONLY to be worn in the house. (That means no, don't run to the car or outside garbage bin in these shoes)

If you are not going to wear a pair of house shoes, then please, please, have your toes nicely manicured (not necessarily French manicure, but filed, cut, and not dry). It is so not cute to walk around with claws for toenails and ashy sandpaper for feet.

Jewelry
A little jewelry goes a long way. Bust out those statement short necklaces, long shiny necklaces, glamorous post earrings, hoop earrings, chunky bangles, skinny stacked bangles, dainty bracelets, gorgeous cocktail rings, even toe rings, and ankle bracelets. A piece or two or three of jewelry will beautifully step up your outfit, so try it!

Makeup

A little lip gloss and eyeliner, eyeshadow, and mascara, maybe some lipstick or a full face if you feel like it can be an elegant enhancement of your natural beauty and complete your look. Not a makeup person? Then just make sure your skin is clean, moisturized, and glowing.

Hair

Do your hair, ladies. It doesn't have to be much. Maybe a cute ponytail, a French braid, hair down with a cute headband, even a scarf in a bun with side bangs if you don't have a lot of time. Whatever you choose, just make sure you do it. Bedhead isn't cute after you're up.

Lingerie

Should I go here? I think I need to. Whether you have a significant other or not, cute undergarments like bras, panties, slips, and robes are necessary. It is okay to feel sexy for yourself. There's something about knowing that you have cute undergarments under your clothes that gives you that extra pep in your step and a good feeling about yourself! :)

CHAPTER 5

FIVE FASHIONABLE MUST-HAVES FOR MOMMIES

As a mommy myself, I understand that our wardrobe may not be the priority anymore. We want to make sure that our children have cute clothes to wear. They are taken care of first, and sometimes we may forget to do the same for ourselves. However, we have to make ourselves and our appearance a priority, too. When you do get a chance to do some shopping for mommy, consider picking up these pieces that will be sure to step up your style.

1) Crossbody Bag

Crossbody bags are always handy, so there are usually plenty of them in stores. Whether it is a fab messenger-style bag, clutch-style, or fringed boho style crossbody, these are a great stylish option for a mommy. You can sling these kinds of bags across your body for hands-free fashion and put you and your child's on-the-go essentials in them. Be sure to pick one that is durable and comfy.

If you want to carry a small crossbody bag, just bring another small bag for the kids' stuff.

If you want to carry a large crossbody bag for both you and the kids' stuff, choose a bag with lots of pockets and organize items with baggies and small pouches.

2) Stylish Sunglasses

Sunglasses are definitely a must-have! They are one of the easiest ways to bump you up in style status and are super helpful for those days when you have tired eyes from a rough night with the little one. No makeup? Not feeling friendly? No problem. Bust out the sunnies!

3) Fabulous Flats

Flats (shoes without height for our purposes) are a fabulous, functional item for a mommy's wardrobe. I'm talking about anything from ballet flats to moccasins and even some suave styles of sneakers. You can chase after a toddler at the playground or do grocery shopping with a good pair of these types of shoes. Get yourself one, two, or even three go-to pairs of cute, quality, comfortable flat shoes that will go with your outfits.

<u>4) Trusty Trench Coat</u>

Trench coats are amazing because you could be wearing the craziest clothing under them, but once you button that jacket up and tie that belt, you are automatically pretty put-together.

If you are in a hurry to get the kids to school and you don't have time to put on a real outfit, just make sure you throw on this trusty piece with real shoes, like a pair of the flats described in #3 (please, no slippers).

<u>5) Hair/Headgear</u>

I'm sure you have had those days when your hair or headscarf was just not cooperating. Throwing on a stylish headband and brushing the rest of your hair down or doing a quick bird's nest style bun is quick and easy. Or, if you are just not in the mood or don't have time for doing your hair or doing up your headscarf at all, just throw a cute hat on (hat on top of the headscarf). There are lots of options out there for hats and hair accessories. Pick one that you love that is relatively versatile, and rock it!

CHAPTER 6

CELEBRATE IN STYLE:
WHAT TO WEAR FOR THE HOLIDAYS

It's that time of year again... when the holidays roll around and you have to find something to wear for those holiday parties and dinners with friends and/or family. Whether you are celebrating Thanksgiving, Eid, Christmas, Kwanzaa, Hanukkah, or other holidays and special events, you should celebrate in style.

What kind of attire is appropriate for the holidays?

Holiday attire can sometimes vary depending on your culture or traditions, but generally, if you wear something formal or even semi-formal, you're good to go. However, *if you are explicitly given a dress code for an event, dress accordingly.* It's bad etiquette and super tacky to come dressed inappropriately to any event, especially if you were told how to dress prior to it by the hosts or on the invite.

The Key

The key to dressing up is to add shine and switch up the fabrics. This is the time to wear those rayon/satins, brocades, jacquards, sequins, and rhinestones on shoes, dresses, skirts, pants, shirts, purses, earrings, etc. in full effect without having to cover it up to keep from looking overdressed.

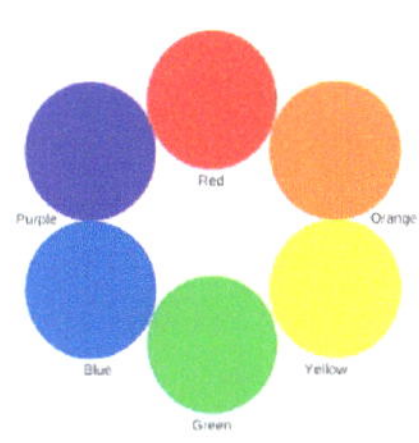

Colors

Color-wise? Color is always in style. To take it up a notch for the holidays, go for all-white, all-black, a metallic-like gold or silver, or rich jewel tones like royal blue, royal purple, crimson, emerald green, etc. paired with bold black to make a striking statement with color.

<u>What are your clothing options?</u>

A skirt and top ensemble, with or without a jacket -
Try a statement top with a subtle skirt or a statement skirt with a subtle top. Don't do too much with BOTH pieces, because the two will compete.

Example:

Yes: A purple bustier-style top with a black pencil skirt.

Yes: A silverish white sequined cardigan with a black straight velvet skirt.

Jacket? Try a jacket to cover up your outfit if you are going from work to a holiday party so that you can switch ensembles/venues without having to stop home to change, want a more modest look, or just to add some extra flavor/shine to our holiday outfit. Anything from blazers to boleros work here. Just be sure to stay away from denim as not to dress your outfit way down.

For hijabis, go with a long skirt and top or jacket in a fancy fabric or texture.

Pantsuit

A pantsuit is one of the most fly things you can wear. Think Bianca Jagger- fly. Choose a statement shirt such as one with ruffles or a rich color to wear with a monochromatic pantsuit to spice it up a little bit with the jacket worn open or closed...and please tailor it to fit your body. There is nothing more terrible than an ill-fitting suit.

For hijabis, try a longer length jacket/blazer in an A-line shape or boyfriend style shape if it is flattering, and that is more your style.

Cocktail Dress

A cheap option if you are on a tight budget this season. Simply wear a cocktail dress or sheath dress that you already have for workwear and dress it up with tights and accessories such as long metallic necklaces, bold bib necklaces, chunky bangles, stacked skinny bangles, a cocktail ring, etc.

Hijabis, some cocktail/sheath dresses can work with a jacket or cardigan of similar length being worn with it along with some pants (not jeans, please).

<u>Pants and Shirt</u>

If you don't feel like wearing a complete suit, then just try some pants in a stylish cut, in a cool fabric like linen or just your regular work pants. Wear it with a great dressy tunic or other statement tops, belted or not belted.

Hijabis, choose a longer length top for a modest look.

<u>The Gown</u>

A long formal dress is probably one of the simplest options out there because the dress makes a big statement, and then all you have to do is accessorize! Find dresses with great details and embellishments like sweetheart necklines, empire waists, and bows or sashes. Bridesmaids and even some styles of prom dresses work very well here.

Hijabis, choose a cute hijab style and add long sleeves if the dress does not already have them. Pair them with a long sleeve shirt, bolero top, cropped cardigan, blazer, or shrug, etc.

Note:

Please, no spaghetti straps on top of long sleeve shirts. It's very tacky. Tuck the straps in or cover them completely with a bolero or shrug.

Skirt Suit

Equally, fly, try a skirt suit. A skirt suit with interesting details such as a peplum jacket or ruffled skirt looks amazing. Try a statement shirt or camisole under the jacket as well. Again, with suits, it's all about FIT. Go to a tailor and make it fit you perfectly to pull this off.

Hijabis, you might be hard-pressed to find a cute skirt suit with a long skirt. But you can always create your own by wearing a straight skirt or other cute cut and pairing it with a tailored jacket.

Cross Cultures

Appreciate another culture this holiday season and try wearing an ensemble that is from a culture different from your own, respectfully. That could mean wearing a beautiful flowing embellished abaya from Dubai, an embroidered Palestinian thoub, an elegant sari or lehenga from the Subcontinent, or a royal three-piece ensemble including headwrap from the Motherland, etc. and spice it up with accessories.

Accessories

Accessories are another great way to dress up an outfit. That's right! Bring out the bling! Glitz it up with faux or real jewels and gems in necklaces, cocktail rings, earrings, hair clips, brooches, and belts.

Hats - a big dramatic hat, or even a small-cap, can add that extra touch to an outfit.

Gloves - Channel Old Hollywood with a fabulous pair of gloves in a great color.

Fur - Don a fur stole tossed around your neck for an even more glamorous look.

Tights - For outfits with legs showing, try a great pair of colored or textured tights.

Purses - This is the time to pull out your dainty purses and leave the huge suitcases and work bags at home. Choose a glittery clutch, dressy chain-strap purse, or even a shiny animal print rectangular wallet will do.

*Check the accessories department in pretty much any clothing store.

Shoes

Step out in style with a gorgeous shoe like a classic black patent peep-toe, a candy-colored stacked heel, or some fabulous metallic flats. Have fun with them and look for great details like bows, jewels, glitter, and animal prints.
Be sure to choose a shoe that will be comfortable to wear so that you don't have to take your shoes off halfway into the party.

Toppers

Keep your whole look classy and beautiful by wearing a great coat! Pieces like tailored trench coats, floor-length fur coats, short patterned coats, capes, and velvet shawls will keep you warm but still dressy.

Note:
Nothing is more tragic than wearing a beautiful outfit and having skin, nails, feet, and hair that look crazy. Make sure your hair is done, your nails are neat, and your feet and skin are moisturized for an utterly fabulous look.

Now, go celebrate in style! :)

THREE WAYS TO STAY A STYLISH MOMMY

Notice the title of this chapter is "... stay a stylish mommy." Sure, you can get a nice makeover, but that is only temporary. For long-term fabulous, you have to keep it up. These three tips can help...

1) Get Rid Of Clothing That Isn't Wearable.

Because if you no longer have it, you can't wear it.

What isn't wearable?

Items that are not wearable are...items that do not fit properly, that do not flatter you, that are in poor condition or items that you simply just do not love.

Yes, it's time to get rid of those jeans that cut off your circulation, that shirt that makes you look pregnant and those beat-up shoes. Bid them all adieu, please. Donate it, sell it, or trash it if necessary.

A functional wardrobe must be 100% wearable, and you should love every single thing in your closet. Imagine how much easier and enjoyable getting dressed would be if everything you owned was fabulous, looked amazing on you, and you actually felt good in it. Yes! That is how it should be.

2) Prepare, Prepare, Prepare!

The key to not looking like a hot mess, even when you are rushing, is preparation. I cannot stress this enough, ladies. You should not have to take forever to get dressed. Taking the time to prepare complete outfits saves time, energy, and guarantees that even if nothing else goes right that day, you will at least look great. Plan outfits (and have hair/hijab style in mind) at least the night before, including clothing, accessories, and shoes, and hang them up in the closet on a hanger (with shoes under) or lay it out on a chair if that is easier - whether it is for work, a special occasion, or even just running errands.

3) Always Go For Fabulous.

When you become a mother, your priorities change...understandably so. You think of the children first most of the time and want them to have the best of everything. However, it is also essential for you to have great things too (not necessarily expensive stuff, just great stuff)! Yes, mommy life is busy, but you don't have to look like you are about to run a marathon all the time. So, go ahead... wear those awesome jeans with the great fit instead of those jogging pants or sweats. Rock those cute ballet flats instead of those sneakers, get that sexy bra, panties, and lingerie instead of that sports bra, granny panty, and flannel pajamas. Purchase that tinted lip gloss or pop lip color instead of the chap stick or lip balm. Take the time to wash your face, moisturize your skin, put on a little makeup if you are in the mood, and please, please do your hair or rock a cute scarf style.

It is easy to put ourselves on the back burner, but it is not healthy for our self-esteem. You need to feel great when you glance at your reflection in the car window or that side mirror where the veggies are in the produce aisle at the grocery store.

Also, as mothers, we can be one of the biggest influences and role models in our children's lives. They need to see that mommy loves herself and is confident and secure.

Not feeling great about your post-baby body? Not at your goal weight? That's okay. These things take time to work on...and that's what Spanx are for.

CHAPTER 8

A TRUSTY NOTE ON TRENDS

My golden rule for trends is: *"You should only participate in trends if they flatter your body type and fit your personal style."*

All trends were not created equal. Some will work for you, some will work for others, and some just don't work for anyone. Sure, a hot turban-style scarf or poppin' pink lip might be all the rage, but if it's not you, don't do it. Stay true to yourself when choosing trends to follow.

Similarly, if you have tummy issues, a drop-waist top is a bad idea, no matter how-of-the-moment it is. Your clothing choices need to flatter your body, always.

Thanks for reading.

Be safe and stylish!

-Hanifah 🖤

ABOUT THE AUTHOR

Hanifah Ashry is a Muslim, New York native and mother of one. She has a background in Fashion Consulting and Early Childhood Education. She enjoys listening to music, cooking, going for walks, reading, and spending time with family and friends.